HISTORIC ROYAL KILRENNY & AN**

CHURCHES, MANSES & SCHOOLS

First published 2001
Copyright of the Kilrenny & Anstruther Burgh Collection
ISBN 0 9536538 1 1
In the same series: Historic Anstruther—People and Places

Edited by Stephanie Stevenson
Contributors: Wilma Anderson, Margaret Darwood, John Dishman, Jennifer Gordon, Dibby Greig, Masry Prince, Peter Prince, Stephanie Stevenson and Rev. Alec Watson
Illustrators: Margaret Darwood, Christine Crowe, Masry Prince and William Stevenson

In 1980 the Anstruther Improvement Association organised an exhibition to show archives, photographs and significant items associated with the Royal Burgh of Kilrenny, Anstruther Easter & Wester. It was felt that the exhibition should be retained and enlarged. Eventually a home was found in the Scottish Fisheries Museum. Later, as the Museum, developed more space was required to house fishing artefacts. The A.I.A. felt unable to manage and store the archives. To resolve this crisis a public meeting was called by Elizabeth Gordon, President of the A.I.A. and Murray Anderson, Chairman of the Community Council. As a result the Burgh Collection was formed under the chairmanship of Alex Darwood. Currently the archives are housed in the Murray Library, where the work of collecting and clarifying material continues.

We are indebted to a grant from the Dalziel Trust towards publication costs

Published by Kilrenny & Anstruther Burgh Collection
Anchor Lodge, St Andrews Road, Anstruther KY10 3HA
Web Site at http://freespace.virgin.net/anstruther.collection/index.htm

CONTENTS

There is a street map at the centre of the booklet, between pages 17 & 18.

Title	Page	Map Reference
Preface	1	
The Early Church, Anstruther & Isle of May	3	1
Kilrenny Church	5	2
Cellardyke Church	8	4
Anstruther Wester Church & Manses	10	6
Anstruther Easter Church & Manse	13	10
James Melville and the old Manse	14	11
Evangelical Church	16	12
Chalmers' Memorial Church	17	13
United Presbyterian Church	19	14
Baptist Church & Manse	20	15
Anstruther Wester School	21	9
Burgh & Free Church Schools	24	17
Kilrenny School	26	3
Cellardyke School	29	5
The Waid Academy	30	18
Vocational Training	32	19
Cultural & Social Activities	34	
Sources		

PREFACE

The story of the church and education in Anstruther and Kilrenny is a small mirror on Scottish history. From the time of St Ninian in the 4th century missionaries from Ireland had brought their Christian message to Scotland. By the end of the 12th century the Church of Rome had largely absorbed these Culdee *(Servant of God)* establishments of the Celtic Church and had organised its own universal system of diocese and parish.

By the 16th century the power and wealth of the Roman Church, the gradual assumption of Church offices and property by royalty and landed laity, the laxity of many monastic houses and priests, the population's consequent lack of spiritual care, together with the influence of continental theologians and economic and political problems, all contributed to the demotion of the Roman Church in Scotland and the adoption of the Reformed Church in 1560.

The Reformed Church had by the end of the 17th century banned the Mass, abolished the authority of the Pope and the hierarchy of the bishops and established a presbyterian system of government with a General Assembly to take the place of the Crown (as in England) as head of the new church.

Education had been a particular concern of the early Church which in most parishes held *little* or *song* schools to train choristers for the church, and grammar schools in cathedrals and most large burghs to educate future clerics and lawyers. In the 15th century three Scottish bishops founded the universities of St Andrews, Glasgow and Aberdeen (Edinburgh received its charter in 1582), which suggests that the provision of education was widespread if not universal.

The reformed church continued to ensure both the moral upbringing of children and a literate population able to read the Bible. Its ambition was a school in every parish but for many years the finances of the church were insufficient for the purpose, though much was achieved. In 1616 an Act of Privy Council commanded every parish to establish a school and in 1633 this was ratified by Parliament with the additional provision that heritors (landowners and proprietors) should be taxed to provide the necessary endowment.

Fee-paying dame schools and adventure schools supplemented parish schools until the 1872 Education Act made schooling compulsory but not free; poor parents could apply to the parochial boards for help. The 1872 Act centralised educational provision set up school boards to manage the schools and insisted that principal teachers held a certificate of competence.

The East of Fife Education Society, set up in 1818, included all schoolmasters along the coast from Elie to Kingsbarns. It met monthly in members' houses, exchanged information on teaching plans and schools visited, and occasionally read essays. It shared a small library and owned chemical and other apparatus.

Private or *Adventure* schools, maintained by pupils' fees, tended to close once the teacher retired or died. Some were privately sponsored as the one at Spalefield set up by Lady Williams of Grangemuir. At one time there was an adventure school for whalers' children in Cellardyke and another in West Forth Street run by Andrew Gourlay, son of the bookseller in Tolbooth Wynd and brother of the author.

As will be seen in the following pages the small burghs of the two Anstruthers and Kilrenny had two pre-reformation churches, two parish schools that were functioning in the 16th and 17th centuries and for over 100 years a secondary school of good repute.

In preparing this book we acknowledge the help of the authors listed in our references and would like thank the staff of the University of St Andrews Library for their help with numerous archive papers also Anne Fairbairn for drawing the map, Joe Fairbairn for technical assistance, John Dishman for typing it on disc and our editor Stephanie Stevenson for steering us through this project. We wish in particular to acknowledge the prompt and willing contributions, *The Early Church in Anstruther, Anstruther Parish Church* and *The Melville Manse*, made by the late, much esteemed, Rev. Alex Watson, minister of Anstruther Parish Church for ten years. We hope others will find as much pleasure in reading the book as we have found in researching and writing it.

THE EARLY CHURCH IN ANSTRUTHER

St Ethernan

The earliest signs of the Christian Mission in this area are associated with the Holy Isle of May and the Caiplie Caves. The man who emerges in this connection is Ethernan, a seventh century monk probably of Irish or Pictish extraction. The choice of an island base is in keeping with the pattern of the Celtic Church of which Columba and Iona are models.

St Ayle

The Crescent and previously the Park (above East Green) take their name from a chapel built in the early fifteenth century. In 1318 land was given to the Cistercian monks of Balmerino Abbey by the de Anstruther family, the occupants of Dreel Castle. The monks built booths there for the local fishermen for drying their nets and for the privilege earned for the Abbey a supply of "the cream of the sea" – salted herring. The name given to the chapel, Agilus or Ayle, is identified with Luxeuil in France and with St Columbanus, an Irish missionary saint and scholar who was educated at Bangor, Co. Down.

The Chapel of St Ayle eventually became a malt barn which was demolished in 1850 and a cooperage was built on the site. A lancet window from the chapel was saved and incorporated in the cooperage which today is in the Scottish Fisheries Museum. The lancet window from the chapel of St Ayle is a feature of the courtyard.

THE ISLE OF MAY

A chapel was dedicated to Ethernan at Kilrenny, anciently spelt Kilretheni – *kil* or chapel of Ethernan and on the Isle of May was a hermitage which remained a holy place after his death in 699 AD.

Subsequently more missionaries, led by Adrian, arrived in Eastern Fife about 832 AD and for some time occupied the Isle of May. Below the Kirkhaven harbour on the island is a raised beach with some divisions of broken stonewalls. Towards the north end of the beach, a little inland, are the ruins of what is called St Adrian's harbour.

According to the fifteenth century breviary of Aberdeen St Adrian was a Hungarian bishop of royal descent. However, most historians think it more likely that he and his company were from Ireland. The caves at Caiplie, between Cellardyke and Crail, are associated with him. There are certain signs of artificial enlargement and early use with incised crosses on the walls. Tradition claims the caves were Adrian's oratory and mainland abode.

At that time there were repeated attacks on the Fife coast by Norse long boats. In 876 AD Constantine, son of Kenneth MacAlpin who joined the Picts and Scots into one kingdom, came to attack the Norsemen near Crail. Constantine was defeated and put to death. Adrian and some of his companions were pursued to the Isle of May and murdered.

So much for tradition; from documented history we know that King David I of Scotland gave the island to the Benedictine Abbey at Reading. A small group of monks was established on the island and by 1153 AD a house had been built. The remains of their chapel and priory can still be seen.

The priory was well endowed by King David and local landowners. The monks owned the manor of Pittenweem, the land of St Monance, pasture in Crail and Kellie, and land further afield, plus a right to all the fish in the water around the May Island. The monks were also responsible for the little church of Anstruther Wester.

In 1288 the monks sold the island for £1,000 to the Bishop of St Andrews. It was then owned by the cathedral of St Andrews, though not without further disputes and litigation. The Isle of May monks moved to their manor at Pittenweem in about 1298. The Priory buildings on the island were despoiled by English invaders and were never restored. The monks continued to harvest the island produce till 1549. They built or rebuilt a hermitage or chapel in memory of St Adrian and other saints. At certain times a priest was on the island to conduct prayers for pilgrims.

The Isle of May was one of Scotland's most noted places of pilgrimage. Mary of Gueldres disembarked there in 1449, before proceeding to Leith to marry James II. James IV was a frequent pilgrim to the island and a generous patron of its hermit and priest.

Just before his death at Flodden in 1513 James IV gave the Isle of May to Sir Andrew Wood of Largo. The island then passed through the ownership of various secular hands till it was sold to the Northern Lighthouse Commission in 1814.

Throughout the 17th and 18th centuries there were residents on the island earning their living by sheep farming and some smuggling; then came lighthouse keepers and their families until the lighthouse was automated, and finally service personnel during the second world war. Anstruther Wester parish included the Isle of May.

In 1958 the Royal Commission for Ancient Monuments officially classified the Priory and ruins on their list, along with the original Beacon stand built in 1636 – the first lighthouse to be built in Scotland. The Isle of May is now under the care of the Nature Conservancy.

KILRENNY CHURCH

Kilrenny Church stands on the hill to the east of Anstruther. The cockerel weather vane at the top of the steeple lost his tail during the great storm that destroyed the Tay Bridge, but he was repaired and replaced, surviving with the same tenacity, as has the church over many centuries. The consecration of an existing church in 1243 was part of the organisation of parishes in Fife; traces of an ancient abbey have been found which are thought to be much older. The Kirk Session was established in 1569 at the time of the reformation: its records show that education, food and money for the poor, and above all the supervision of the conduct of parishioners were the abiding concerns of the ministers and elders. *The pair guilty of adultery were to be rebuked three several Sabbath days in the church* while sitting on the stool of repentance…*they must submit to Discipline so they may be restored to Christian privileges.*

In November 1806 the structure of the church was in a poor state: *all publick worship at Kilrenny is to be discontinued until the*

Kilrenny Church and Church Hall, formerly Kilrenny School

roof be repaired and declared in a safe and sufficient state. The kirk was rebuilt, little other than the old steeple remaining. The old kirk had been wholly paved with gravestones, although burial within the church had ceased before 1600...*the human bones are generally in regular order about 14 in the space below the flags to a depth of 5 or 6 feet.* The bones were removed. The new kirk was opened in 1806. A few years later the heritors were *satisfied of the ruinous state of the manse,* which was on the lower part of the kirkyard by the bridge, *and unanimous that a new manse must be built.* It was built on the other side of the Crail Road.

Visitors will see that a tablet on the south wall commemorates seven generations of the Williamson family who worshipped in the kirk. Archibald Williamson, ship owner, was one of the managers of the parish during a prolonged period of disfranchisement from 1829 until 1867; the result of suspicions of corrupt practices in the election of councillors and magistrates. This purely secular dispute affected the kirk as there was no representation at the General Assembly.

Many ministers served for long periods. Mr Anderson died in 1925 having been inducted in 1878. The Rev. John Marshall Pryde, a former army padre, succeeded him. He found box pews, no choir or organ and in the old tradition a precentor, Sandy Reid, who led the singing armed with a tuning fork. Mr Pryde had a water organ installed and established a choir.

Extensive repairs became necessary in 1930. After the

reformation the communion table had been taken from the 'altar-wise' position at the east end, held to be reminiscent of 'popish practises', and placed centrally. The pulpit and table were now placed at the east end and the gallery, which formerly ran along three walls, was placed at the west end. At the cost of £20 a new pulpit, pews and reredos were acquired from a church in St Andrews. St Marys, which closed in 1921 and was later reconstructed as the Victory Memorial Hall. The opportunity to purchase the stained glass windows was not taken.

 Mr and Mrs Pryde suffered the loss of three sons during the second world war, all pilots in the Royal Air Force. In spite of this it is remembered that Mr Pryde never missed a service.

 The Rev. Hamish MacNab was inducted as minister in 1947. During his ministry the old school building, now the church hall, was extended by the addition of a lounge built by parishioners. The disused Session House, the foundations of which can be seen to the right of the kirk gate, was dismantled to provide stones for this work.

 The visitor will find many distinctive memorials in the kirkyard including the burial ground of the Anstruther family and many headstones telling of tragedies at sea. The Lumsdaine Memorial, attached to the west end of the kirk, commemorates a family who lived for many years at nearby Innergellie House. At the north western corner there is a memorial to General John Scott raised by his great-great grandson, Lord Howard de Walden. General Scott, who owned estates at Scotstarvit and Balcomie acquired his wealth by gambling. He successfully staked £30;000 in a game with Sir Lawrence Dundas who staked his house in St Andrews Square, Edinburgh. Dundas retained the house, which is now owned by the Bank of Scotland, but built an equivalent mansion for Scott. His three daughters, heiresses of great wealth, became Countess of Moray, Duchess of Portland, and Viscountess Canning.

 The parishes of Kilrenny and Cellardyke were linked in 1988 on the retirement of the Rev. MacNab. The old Kilrenny manse was sold into private ownership. The Cellardyke manse now houses the minister.

CELLARDYKE CHURCH

In 1877 the minister of Kilrenny, the Rev. John Christie D.D., said that a new church should be built within the parish to accommodate the growing population. Mr Philip Oliphant, banker and writer (lawyer), took a leading part in the collection of money for this purpose. The church was built on land purchased from Mr Charles Bethune of Balfour and opened in 1881. Two ministers served briefly as missionaries and when in 1883 the church was established as a 'quoad sacra' parish within the parish of Kilrenny the Rev. James Ray was inducted as the first minister. The success of his ministry of 34 years can be gauged by the increase of his congregation from 40 to over 700. The manse was built at the top of Toll Road in 1887. Mr Ray married Philip Oliphant's daughter in 1888. He was called to a kirk in Portobello in 1917 and was followed by the Rev. James Lee from Invergarry, minister until 1951, when he died. He was followed by the Rev. James Matthews, who eventually retired in 1982. Thus the parish was served by three ministers during its first 99 years. Each of these men is commemorated by fine stained glass windows in the church.

Cellardyke Church

The long serving ministers have been matched by the kirk organists. There have been three from 1905: Miss Robina Oliphant (1905-1935), Mr William Blair (1935-1978) and Mr Robert Gardner from 1978 to the present day. The first organist, Miss Oliphant, was paid £25 pa which she asked should be used for the upkeep of the organ, any remaining to be put into an endowment fund.

The font inscribed to the memory of Philip Oliphant was presented to the church after his death in 1893 and a fine new organ installed in 1905 at a cost of £600, replacing a harmonium. Dr Andrew Carnegie of Skibo Castle contributed £300 towards its purchase. As a memorial a communion table bearing the names of members of the congregation who had fallen in the first world war was presented, together with seven fine chairs.

A hall was built at the east end of the kirk in 1927, paid for in part by fund-raising by the congregation. Eventually this was seen to be inadequate and in 1970 work was set in train to build a larger hall with a new suite of rooms. The many willing tradesmen in the congregation, joiners, plumbers and slaters, worked in the evenings and on Saturdays, while the ladies supplied tea and biscuits. The work was expected to take three years, it took two. The people of Cellardyke paid for all the materials, provided at cost by local firms. This communal effort was a splendid reflection of the exceptionally loyal spirit within Cellardyke.

Cellardyke Manse

ANSTRUTHER WESTER CHURCH AND MANSES

Parishes were first introduced into Scotland in the 12th century and among the earliest was the parish of Anstruther Wester. In a list of priests' stipends in 1177 Anstruther's was 10 merks compared with Kilrenny's 26 and Abercrombie's 6. On 28th June 1243 the parish church was dedicated to a saint of the Roman Church, St Nicholas. James IV on his way to the Isle of May in June 1503 landed at Anstruther to say a mass and in June 1559 John Knox preached here. We know from Kirk Session records that the building had conformed to the usual pattern of a Catholic church: *the remains of a large choir, Kirk Ayles* or aisles, windows in the *high stories* or clerestory and *rows of fine arches*; other than this little is known about Anstruther Wester's early church. Until 1588 the parish included Pittenweem.

Anstruther Wester Church

In about 1560 William Clark was appointed the first Protestant minister of Anstruther, Abercrombie, Pittenweem and Kilrenny. For a time he lived in the house now known as Chalmers' Birthplace. In 1586 the Rev. James Melville was appointed minister to the four churches after the death in 1583 of William Clark, of whom Melville wrote that he was *the light and lyff in the part he dwelt in, mikle belovit and regretted of all sorts of persones that knew him*, and after the short incumbency of Robert Wood whom the bishop of St Andrews had *obtrudit* to the congregation *of whom they liked nathing*. Melville brought with him his brother-in-law and *faithful frind and companion* Robert Dury, to whom he resigned in 1588 the *church of Anstruther, gleib and manse*, himself retaining the parish of Kilrenny.

The church was in constant need of repair and finally in 1845 it was *entirely modernised* and increased in size, for the third time, to its present dimensions. There were twenty ministers of the Wester parish church between 1560 and 1958, several of them staying for over 30 years, and two for 50 years and more. The Rev. Andrew Burn, first occupant of the new 1703 manse, died in 1760 *Father of the Synod of Fife* after 58 years in the parish. The Rev. Hew Scott, author of *Fasti Ecclesiae Scoticanae*, a record of all the parish ministers of the Church of Scotland, who died in 1872, was minister for 33 years. The much loved James Paterson, the last minister, served for 50 years.

By the mid-twentieth century the congregation had so dwindled that on April 23rd 1961 at a service in the Easter Anstruther parish church the Rev. Wilfred Hulbert, Moderator of the Presbytery of St Andrews, announced the union of the Easter and Wester parishes under the name of "Anstruther St Adrian".

The Manses

The manse that was resigned to the Rev. Robert Dury in 1588 is not now identifiable but in the 18th century there was a single-storey house on the south side of the churchyard which was always referred to in title deeds as those *Cellars... lately occupied by the Parish Minister* or as *the Minister's Cellars*. This single-storey building was later let for storage until 1867 when the heritors sold it. It was rebuilt and is now known as *Dolphin Cottage*.

The heritors built a new manse across the road in 1703. By the 1830s it was thought to be damp and incommodious but it continued to be occupied, as it still is. Forbes MacGregor, author of *Salt Sprayed Burgh*, often stayed there.

Anstruther Wester Manse, built in 1703

In 1835-6 the heritors built a new manse on the Kirk's two-acre glebe on the Pittenweem Road. It was the first substantial house to be built In 1835-6 the heritors built a new manse on the Kirk's two-acre glebe on the Pittenweem Road. It was the first substantial house to be built beyond the limits of the old burgh and for a small poor parish it was indeed substantial. The first occupants were the Rev. Andrew Carstairs and his family of twelve but he died two years later. It was then occupied by the Rev Hew Scott, who had no children. The manse *on a large scale in every respect* was put up for sale in 1961 but failed to find a buyer. Demolition was suggested but it was ideal for the late Mr Eddie Clarke's purpose: he was looking for a suitable building to start a hotel. The manse, renamed *The Craw's Nest Hotel* was opened in 1963.

Until Melville's Manse in East Anstruther was restored in 1977 and ready for occupation, a house in Pittenweem Road built in 1915 by Robert Boyter, now the *Grange Guest House*, was rented as a manse for the new minister of the combined parishes, the Rev. Charles Miller.

ANSTRUTHER EASTER KIRK AND MANSE

Land to build a church in Anstruther Easter was purchased in 1592 through the initiative of James Melville, minister at Kilrenny. The ground chosen was a *lovely spot where the children used to gather flowers of spring*. The motivation for acquiring the site was Melville's concern that the people of Anstruther Easter, in particular the infirm and elderly, had to make their way to Kilrenny Church - *a mile distant of deep evil way in winter and rainy times*. Events in London prevented Melville from overseeing the building of the church and it was left to his successor at Kilrenny to see to it. It was completed in 1634 and Colin Adam, minister at Kilrenny, left his charge to become the first parish minister of the new charge. It was a specially created parish being coterminous with the burgh which made it the smallest parish in Scotland. It is a barnlike building without apse or chancel.

Anstruther Easter Church, now the Parish Church

The steeple was an after-thought, being built to house a *siller bell* made by a Danish bell-founder in Stockholm. An inscription on the bell reads *Andro Strang bougt this bell with his owne moneyes anno 1641*.

The oldest feature inside the church is on the south wall: the tomb of Master John Dykes, called to assist James Melville in 1596. He died when the church was being built and so was buried inside the church.

In 1905 a major enrichment of the church took place: the instillation of two stained glass windows, the St Peter in memory of Rev. Thomas Murray and the St Philip in memory of Charles and Elizabeth Gray, Nareeb, Victoria, Australia. In 1938 the remaining four side lights were filled with stained glass by Mrs Logan in memory of her brothers Robert Black, who was lost at sea, and John Black. Mrs Logan was the daughter of Dr Thomas Black, who was drowned while out on a mission of mercy at the harbour on 29th February 1864 at the age of 46. His portrait hangs in the Town Hall and there is in the Anstruther Church graveyard an eloquent memorial consisting of a broken column with a coronet of flowers.

Anstruther Easter Church, interior

JAMES MELVILLE AND THE OLD MANSE

James Melville, son of the minister of Marytown near Montrose, was born in 1556. His uncle, Andrew Melville, for many years leader of the Scottish Presbyterians, became in 1580 Principal of St Mary's College, St Andrews. The same year James became Professor of Hebrew and Oriental Languages at the University.

James is famous for his *Autobiography and Diary*, a treasury for historians. One of the very special events recorded concerns the arrival on 6th December 1558 of Spaniards from the ill-fated Armada in Anstruther Wester where James Melville was minister prior to his call to the parish of Kilrenny. Their ship, *El Gran Griffon* had been driven by storms against the cliffs of the Fair Isle between Orkney and Shetland. After spending some months on Fair Isle a boat was bought from the Shetlanders in order to return to Dunkirk which was then occupied by Spain. The craft proved to be unseaworthy and was forced to put into Anstruther. The *Diary* describes Don Jan Gomez de Medina, commander of 20 Armada galleons, as a *verie reverend man of big stature, grey-bearded and verie humble lyk. Bowing down with his face neir the ground* he besought James Melville for help with food and accommodation for which, to thank him on leaving Anstruther a few days later, Don Jon gave the minister the ship's pay chest.

When the manse was built two years later largely by James' efforts the pay chest was installed above the study door. It has been suggested that although there is no available evidence, the contents of the chest helped to fund the building of the manse. The *Diary* refers to the manse as a *spectackle of God's libertie*. Was the pay chest placed, so significantly, above the study door by Melville as an icon of God's gracious goodness?

Melville's *The Watch Tower* is inscribed on a panel on the gable of the south jamb. As a Hebrew scholar he would have been familiar with the Old Testament prophet Habukkuk who saw himself in a watch tower keeping an eye on events for God, an office to which the builder of the Manse would have readily aspired.

James I & VI summoned Melville to London for his Presbyterian convictions and principles in 1606 and sent him into ward at Newcastle. On his way back to Edinburgh in 1614 he died at Berwick.

Since James Melville had put so much into the building of the manse he regarded it as his own property and willed it to his family who continued to live in it until his grandson Ephraim sold it to Sir William Anstruther in 1637. In May 1679 Archbishop Sharp, formerly minister at Crail, visited the family and stayed overnight. Next day he was murdered as he travelled via Magus Muir from Ceres to St Andrews. As a tribute to the Archbishop the Anstruther family installed a plaster cast replica of the murder scene in Holy Trinity Church in St Andrews. The replica is displayed in what was James Melville's study.

Mostly widow members of the Anstruther family occupied the former manse until 1717 when it became the property of the town and once more a manse for the minister. In the grounds there is an ancient well and a 17th century square-roofed dovecot containing 291 nests all of solid dressed stone built into the massive walls.

THE EVANGELICAL CHURCH

Chalmers' birthplace, Old Post Office Close, which was bought by a local writer in 1792 was inherited by his daughter who in 1848 sold it to her aunt, Agnes Robb, who ran the Post Office there. Agnes was married to the Rev. John Murdoch *late of Blackburn Academy, Lancashire*, who after six months labour in Anstruther was ordained pastor of the Congregational Church in 1830.

Scottish Congregationalism owes its beginning to the Scottish brothers Robert and James Haldane who as evangelical preachers toured the country at the end of the 18th century trying to rouse the somnolent church. Their failure to do so convinced them of the need to form a voluntary fellowship of autonomous local churches, the Congregational Union of Scotland.

The Congregational Church in Anstruther was formed in about 1830 and met in a weaver's shop in East Green known locally as the *Tabernacle*. It was unsuitable for a place of worship as it was too small and frequently overcrowded, but the Baptists retained it when the Congregationalists built a new chapel in the new Crail Road at a cost of £400. Most of the £250 already collected towards the cost of the building at the time of its opening on 26th November 1833 was collected by John Murdoch from Christian friends in various parts of the country.

John Murdoch continued as pastor until 1844 when most of the congregation adopted Evangelical opinions. He and a remnant of the congregation vacated the building and held meetings in the old Town House in Shore Street until Murdoch removed to Lerwick. In 1865 he was in Portobello where his son witnessed John's sale of Chalmers' Birthplace.

The Evangelical Church in Crail Road continued in use until about 1916. It is now used as a warehouse by Grey & Pringle.

CHALMERS MEMORIAL CHURCH

The story of this much loved church is intertwined with the history of the Scottish nation. After the sensational Disruption in May 1843, when the Free Church seceded from the Established Church, a building programme of churches, manses, schools and schoolhouses immediately commenced, due entirely to the leadership of Anstruther's most famous son, Dr Thomas Chalmers, Moderator of the new Free Church.

The first Kirk Session meeting of the new congregation in Anstruther was held on June 13th 1843, under the direction of the minister, the Rev. William Fernie, who had left the Parish Church at the Disruption. Two days later plans for the building of their first church were discussed. The building was a temporary structure and was replaced in 1859 by another church designed by John Milne, a St Andrews architect. This was an imposing building in pointed Gothic style with a vestry and heating apparatus. The cost was £800 and the minister was Rev. Alexander Gregory. He was succeeded by his assistant, the Rev. Alexander McAlpine, who was minister when the third and final church was built in 1891.

Plans for this church were mooted in 1888 when Stephen Williamson, MP for St Andrews and a distinguished Cellardyke man, purchased land for the site. Later he contributed £2273 towards the building costs and on the 12th April 1890 he laid the foundation stone. He also gave the church a *handsome manse* (his late parents' house, *Bellfield* in School Green) and a house for the beadle, 3 Union Place, as well as a grand pipe organ to be built by Wadsworth Brothers of Manchester and Aberdeen. In addition Mr Williamson donated all the stained glass windows.

The architect of this striking edifice was David Hendry FSA (Scotland). It was constructed of pointed stone resting on cast iron pillars and was inspired by the example of Dunblane Cathedral. The majestic tower and spire rose to 140 feet and was situated in the north west corner of the nave. The boarded ceiling was 45 feet high. Some 170 tons of stone quarried at Spynie quarry, near Elgin, were brought by two steamers from Lossiemouth to Anstruther Harbour. The roofs were

1. St Ayles (Early Church in Anstruther)
2. Kilrenny Church
3. Kilrenny School
4. Cellardyke Church
5. Cellardyke School
6. Anstruther Wester Church
7. Anstruther Wester Manse (1703)
8. Anstruther Wester Manse (*The Craws Nest*)
9. Anstruther Wester School
10. Anstruther Easter Church
11. Anstruther Easter Manse
12. Evangelical Church
13. Chalmers Memorial Church
14. United Presbyterian Church
15. Baptist Church and Manse
16. Burgh School
17. Free Church School
18. Waid Academy
19. Technical School

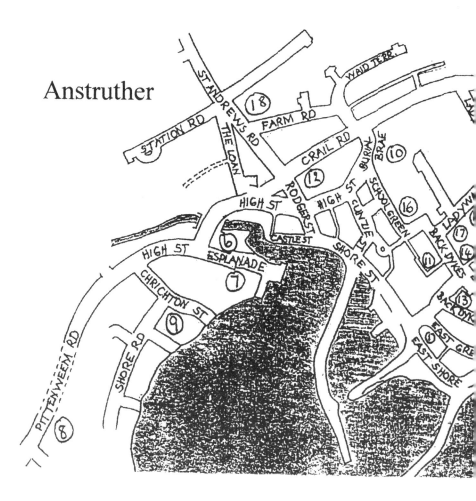

Anstruther

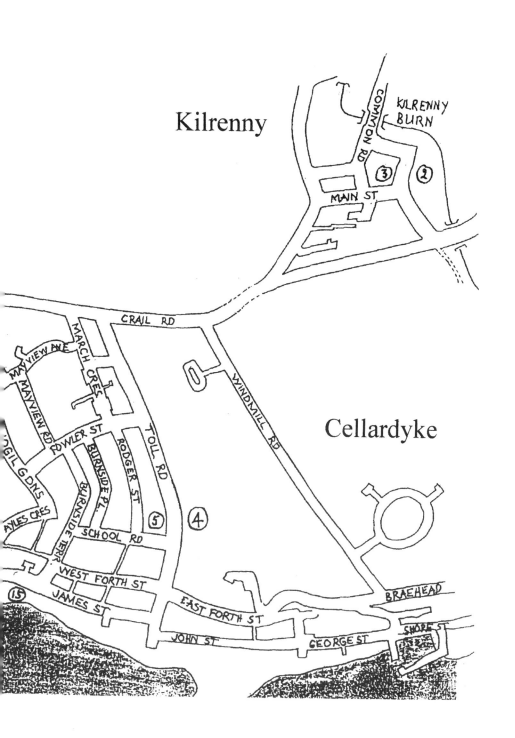

clad in green slate from north Wales. The interior was well designed and spacious. At the east end was a vestry, session house and attractive hall with service kitchen. A notable feature of the church was a series of stained glass medallions in the windows, each portraying a famous ecclesiastical martyr or reformer, from St Columba to Martin Luther, John Calvin, John Knox, Andrew and James Melville and, of course, Thomas Chalmers. These medallions, glazed with cathedral glass in lead mounts, were created by Messrs Ballantine of Edinburgh. When illuminated from behind their rich colours were strikingly beautiful.

Chalmers' Memorial Church

The first service in the new church was held on 13th May 1891 and was conducted by the Rev. J.H.Wilson of the Barclay Church Edinburgh. The church continued to thrive and prosper and became a leading spiritual force in the Burgh. In 1929 the Free Church reunited with the Established Church. Sadly however, like congregations throughout the country numbers began to decline in the mid 20th century and in 1973 it was decided to link Chalmers'

Church with St Adrians, not an easy decision. Finally in 1983 Chalmers' Memorial Church was closed for good.

Despite various attempts to find a use for the deserted building it remained in an increasing state of dereliction until May 1991 when fire totally gutted the magnificent edifice. The remaining walls, including the great spire, were demolished on 13th May exactly 100 years to the day since the opening ceremony. A few relics were rescued, including the six and a half cwt bell. Poignantly, as the fire burned through the rope, the bell in falling, tolled as it had done on the joyous opening day in 1891. The church, sited on the highest point of the town presented a remarkably dominant but endearing image which meant so much to townspeople and visitors alike. To countless fishermen returning from hazardous voyages it signified home and safety. To this day it is sadly missed.

THE UNITED PRESBYTERIAN CHURCH

The United Presbyterian Church was founded in 1847 by a union of seceders from the Church of Scotland. The first or *Original Secession* in 1733 was led by Ebenezer Erskine (1650-1754) one time minister at Portmoak, when he was suspended at Stirling for giving a sermon defending the claims of congregations to elect their own ministers.

The Anstruther UP Church in Back Dykes, built with 400 sittings at a cost of £860, was opened for worship in February 1852. The manse in Ladywalk (now Brackness House) was built in 1860, largely at the expense of the minister.

The Church became the joint Sunday School after the union of the UP and Free Churches in 1900. In 1938 the staff of the Labour Exchange in the High Street moved into the building. Forty years later it was bought by a Manchester clothing firm, who for two years had rented an outbuilding at the Anstruther holiday camp and it became known locally as the *shirt factory,* with 15 women employed full-time making ladies blouses.

When the firm was dissolved the former church was eventually taken over by the Regional Council and was opened in August 1994 as an annex to the East Neuk Centre as the *Erskine Hall.*

THE BAPTIST CHURCH AND MANSE

The Baptist Church is situated at the east end of East Green at the very edge of the sea; in stormy weather the waves come crashing over the boundary walls.

There are three dissenting meeting-houses in this parish – Burgher, Independent and Baptist reported the 1845 New Statistical Account. The Baptist meeting-house was somewhere in East Green and about 33 families of the Anstruther parish were members.

The Baptist Church and Manse

An advertisement in the *East of Fife Record* of 10th March 1860 called for builders' estimates for the construction of a chapel and Vestry at East Green, Anstruther; it was completed (surely in record time) by the 4th November when the opening service took place. Baptist ministers from Kirkcaldy, Perth and Edinburgh attended with a large congregation. Mr James Morris, the builder was presented with a *beautifully bound copy of Dr Chalmers' Memoirs*. Sacred music was provided by the choir of the Independent Church of Elie. The ceremony ended at about 10 pm with a *handsome collection of £52 odd plus £20 promised from 'a distant land'*.

In December an article praised the building as *elegant and chaste…the best looking public building we have in the place, both externally and internally, though it is a pity it is not in a more commanding site…The water tank used for immersion when the Ordinance of Baptism is observed is not visible at other times, being sunk below the floor level, with a wooden covering.*

Accommodation for the minister and his family was provided at the west end of the church with a separate entrance from the adjacent wynd, but in 1874 a solid sandstone villa was built as a manse by Hall & Henry of St Andrews in the newly developed area of St Ayle's Park. The Rev. Peter Buchan Noble lived there from 1902 until 1923; *handsome, blue-eyed, red-haired*, he was a good amateur artist and a clarinet player. He married Jessie Mitchell, daughter of David Mitchell, sailmaker in Rodger Street. Under Noble the Church flourished, the Sunday school having at one time 100 regular pupils.

The manse was sold in 1970 and the minister once more accommodated in the upper flat of the Baptist Church by the sea.. Latterly there has been no regular resident minister, but on 27th May 2000 the Rev. Alasdair Nicholl was inducted into his new charge, with hopes for the future of the Baptist ministry in Anstruther.

ANSTRUTHER WESTER SCHOOL

In 1575 the Kirk Session of Anstruther Wester, following the precepts of John Knox and the Protestant reformers, thought it meet that all the youth in the town should be caused to come to the school *and sic as are puir shall be furnished upon the common expense.*

The school met in the church tower until the Act of 1696 required the heritors to provide a schoolhouse and salary for the schoolmaster. Until 1718 the Session House on the south side of the kirkyard was taken in tack for the school which was closed for a time in 1700 *both upon account of the indisposition of the minister and the poverty of the place.* The schoolmaster's salary in 1794 was £8 6s 8d a year with *10 merks a year from the Session for teaching poor children.* He was esteemed the best teacher of navigation on the coast and *all the young people in the parish without exception are taught to read English, and the principles of the Christian religion.* When the new Town Hall was built in 1794 the heritors rented the ground floor for the school until 1827.

By that time the ground floor was found to be *very deficient in accommodation* and as the schoolmaster was aged and infirm and pupils were attending neighbouring parish schools the heritors built a substantial new school in 1831 at the corner of Shore Road and Crichton Street at a cost of £400 15s 3d.

In 1838 reading, writing, arithmetic, geography, Latin,

French, algebra and pure and practical mathematics were taught with fees from 10s to £1 5s a year *according to the age or attainments of the children.* The parishioners in general seemed to be fully alive to the benefits of education, *even the very poorest make considerable exertions to procure education for their children.* A photograph shows the new Wester School as an oblong, single-storey stone building with large sash windows and a school bell on the slate roof. A house and garden was provided for the schoolmaster.

In 1878 elected school boards replaced the supervision of the heritors and the Session, but the heritors still had to pay the salary of the schoolmaster who himself paid for pupil teachers and an assistant out of the fees he collected from parents. On 17th March 1875 the elected School Board organised the cleaning, painting and repairing of the school and in August conferred with other schools on vacation dates. They appointed Jessie Dougall, daughter of the schoolmaster, as a pupil teacher provided she passed her examinations, with a salary of £10, increasing by £2 10s for the succeeding four years. Her mother was appointed to teach sewing and cutting two hours each day for £5 a year with a fee of 1d a week from each scholar taking the subject. In winter children had to pay coal money.

The Board interviewed parents of pupils who were too often absent; their frequent excuse was that they could not afford the fees. In November 1874 local residents protested to the Board that most of them, relying on their labour for income, were being asked to pay *a rate four or five times that of the well-to-do tenant of land.*

Anstruther Wester School, demolished 1951

Miss Jessie Storm was appointed assistant in 1875 at £50 a year to teach, beside ordinary lessons, "Industrial Management" to girls which by 1881 ranged from sewing to laundrywork.

By 1879 there were 149 on the school roll of whom 19 were taught free and 15 were under 6 years of age.

The Inspector reported in May 1881 *that domestic industry was well attended to*; subjects taught were reading, grammar, composition, history, geography and arithmetic, but the last was not satisfactory in the 5th and 6th grades where there were 36 failures out of 63.

David Findlay from Glasgow was appointed assistant master in September 1881 at £70 a year. When in June 1882 Mr Dougall gave notice of his impending retirement Findlay and William V. Wilson of Pittenweem, teacher in Leven, both applied for his job. The Board offered the post to Findlay with an emolument of £15 on his current salary, but he would have to pay a pupil teacher and an ex-pupil teacher. Mr Findlay declined the offer. The Clerk replied that the Board did not see their way to improving their offer *and that his services as an assistant will not be required after three months*. The job was offered to Wilson who accepted it. David Findlay, however did better: when Miss Maggie Fordyce of Anstruther Wester was appointed assistant at £30 a year she came with a testimonial from the Anstruther Easter schoolmaster – David Findlay!

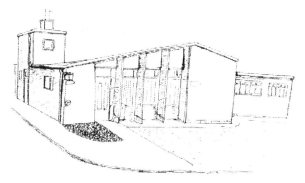

Anstruther Wester Primary School

In October 1882 Mr Wilson required from the Board: a new set of maps, a set of object lessons in the animal kingdom, a sheet for teaching form and colour, and a set of school books for his own use, and he wished to be reimbursed for the purchase of a modulator (a tonic sol-fa chart) and a set of writing sheets. The 1888 Inspector reported *a very creditable knowledge of History and Geography... Singing is good, and Domestic Industry is satisfactory.*

After 3 years Mr Wilson and Miss Fordyce were both registered as certificated teachers, a period required for certification well into the 1930s.

The school was demolished in 1951 and replaced by the present primary school at a cost of £20,177.

THE BURGH SCHOOL AND FREE CHURCH SCHOOL

In the old burgh the schoolroom was housed in the Tolbooth, alongside the jail, courts and meeting place of the Town Council, which was built in the 17th century at the foot of Tolbooth Wynd, Shore Street. By 1719 the schoolhouse in Tolbooth Wynd was occupied by soldiers serving at the Customs House and the Burgh School moved to what is now the workshop of Murray and Wilson in School Green.

The Statistical Account for Scotland of 1845 found this to be the only school in the parish of Anstruther Easter teaching reading, writing, arithmetic, geography and occasionally Latin. At this time the number of pupils attending averaged eighty. As a Burgh school the teacher was appointed by the town council which paid his salary of £5 8s 8d pa. Two notable Mortifications (a bequest to some charitable institution, under Scots law), left by a Mr Henderson and Andrew Walker, sometime Banquier in Paris, paid the equivalent of £7 sterling pa to the schoolmaster of the parish.

The Burgh School also offered classes in religious knowledge and the shorter catechism. Mr Cruikshank, headmaster in 1846, had an annual salary with the Henderson fund and government allowances of £169 9s 6d.

Notable ex-pupils of the Burgh School include the *Anster Fair* poet and professor of Oriental Languages at St Andrews University, William Tennant; the distinguished anatomist John Goodsir, eldest son of the local surgeon; the successful sons of the merchant, Philip Paton, the eldest of whom became an admiral in the Royal Navy in 1805; the decorated Captain James Black of the HMS *Weasel* and his brother Rear

Admiral William Black who at his death in Norfolk in 1852 left money to pay for the education of poor children in the parish of Anstruther Easter, and Thomas Chalmers, leader of the Disruption of the Church of Scotland in 1843.

One of Chalmers' life long convictions was that Church and Education were inseparable. It was not then surprising that sufficient funds were raised to build and open in November 1846, only 3 years after the founding of the Anstruther Free Church, a new school at the junction of Back Dykes and Ladywalk. In that year a census of children between the ages of 5 and 13 showed that 133 pupils attended the Burgh School and 60 the Free Church School. Miss Gordon's Seminary in East Green was included with 16 pupils on the roll.

Robert Smith from Glasgow was appointed first master of the Free Church School to teach *the higher branches including Latin, French, algebra, history, geography, etc.* A Miss Buick, who gave instruction in the domestic arts such as knitting and sewing, taught the girls. A five-apartment schoolhouse (now the rates office) was built next to the school in 1859.

School inspections of 3 hours were carried out by the St Andrews Free Church Presbytery Committee attended by a large gathering of parents and friends and *many influential inhabitants of the town and neighbourhood..* The HM Inspector of Schools was *much gratified with the successful teaching* and expressed *unqualified approval of the results.*

In the 1850s and '60s the Free Church ministers drew many people to lectures, which were subsequently published, in the new schoolroom on Sunday afternoons. At this time there were 180 boys and 116 girls at the school to which Stephen Williamson donated a gift of £100 in 1872.

The following year, 1873, a School Board was established in Anstruther Easter parish and in July the Free Church agreed to hand over to it the running of its school which subsequently became known as the East Public School while the Burgh School became the West Public School. Responsibilities of the School Board included the hiring of cleaners: in September Widow Robertson of Kirk Wynd was hired to clean the school and light the fire daily for a payment of £3 a year.

The West School was less well attended than the former Free Church School which in April 1874 reported overcrowding. On the sudden death of Mr Cruikshank in November it was proposed to turn the West School into an Infant School for the under sevens. Responses in 1875 to the advertisement for a teacher of the Infant School came from as far as East Grimsby and Patcrieff near Manchester!

The Free Church School

By the end of the 19th century the two schools proved inadequate and work began on a new school at the west end of Melville Terrace. In 1901 the new elementary school was opened and the former Free Church School was sold to the Volunteers as a Drill Hall (now the East Neuk Community Centre). The new school became part of the Waid in the 1920s and all children since attend either Anstruther Wester or Cellardyke Schools before going to the Waid at the age of 12. A new primary school for the whole town is currently being planned on a site adjoining the Waid Academy.

KILRENNY SCHOOL

Kilrenny School was from time immemorial and up to 9th September 1878 the principal school of the parish....thus a petition to oppose closure in 1891 over 115 signatures. The date refers to the opening of Cellardyke School. Kilrenny School for long educated the children of a large parish under the aegis of the kirk with the often grudging support of the heritors. There is little record of the school before the reformation, but Kirk Session records after 1560 are informative.

Only those who *professed Christ's trew religion* were

admissible as teachers, those who were able to inculcate *godliness and gud maners.* At the reformation the many holy days... *superstitious and popish practises...* were removed, but scholars were permitted to enter their cocks for the cockfights on Fasten's E'en (Shrove Tuesday evening) before the Lenten fast. The tradition of ignoring Christmas continued into the 20th century; as late as 1913 the school closed for the New Year's vacation on Friday 26th December. Summer and autumn vacations were allowed; the children of the poor being needed for the harvest. For reading and writing the Bible was the main textbook. The catechism was learnt by heart and much else by rote. The duty of the master was to make and mend pupils' pens, take inspection of every writing and control a large number of pupils with the aid of a 'captain', a pupil chosen to report on the misbehaviour of his fellows. The tawse was used, but the magistrates and the Kirk Session usually prevented excessive punishment.

In 1598 the Privy Council ordered *masters of colleges to give liberty to pupils in their pastimes after 12 o'clock on Mondays.* By 1665 schools *give play to scholars on Tuesdays, Thursdays and Saturdays,* but the schoolmaster at Kilrenny gave more than *the ordinary days,* to the dissatisfaction of the Kirk Session.

Days were long in Fife schools in 1665, 7-9 am, 10am to noon, and 2-6pm. On Sundays the children went to school and then sat in the scholars' loft in the kirk. After this the sermon had to be summarised for the master's inspection.

Times at school were often shortened in the winter, which brought foul paths and swollen streams. The children of Cellardyke were kept home in 1651 *until the days grew longer and the way better.* These children were young. In 1647 the Synod decreed that school life should last for at least 5 years, from 6 to 11.

The schoolmaster was paid a salary and also received fees from the scholars, who paid *their quarter payment at the entries.* The Kirk Session paid the expenses of poor scholars. If some children went to adventure, that is privately run, schools the schoolmaster lost his fees. When in 1653 he complained that *thair came not a boy out of Sillerdykes to the school* the Kirk Session forbade the use of adventure schools.

In 1700 there were long hours of attendance during which there was concentration on doctrine, behaviour and *teaching the gramer.* Hours eventually became shorter. In 1750 the new master was tried in the Roman authors, writing and arithmetic. In the 19th century Mr Dalrymple was required to teach English grammar, reading, history, geography, mathematics, navigation, Latin and French for £35 pa. The female teacher taught some of these subjects with plain sewing and knitting in addition for £12 pa. The scholars did not usually attempt all subjects.

The life and work of the Master was regularly reviewed on Presbyterial visititations. These could be painful. The Master's appointment could be terminated for 'bad conduct'. Mr Harry Page was dismissed in 1649, but on showing himself *trulie penitent* he was reinstated as Master and Session Clerk. Again in 1861 the master was sacked – unfit for office due to addiction to drink.

The school was probably housed in a plain stone building of two storeys with the schoolroom above and the Master living below. Several groups would be taught together, master and doctor (assistant master) holding forth at the same time. In the 1870s scholars paid 1d a month to pay for cleaning and heating.

During the 19th century a Compulsory Officer threatened parents with prosecution if children failed to attend school. Betsy Smith kept her children at home because they had no shoes. She was directed to apply to the Inspector of Poor for assistance. There were many such cases.

Although a new school was built in Cellardyke in 1878 a proposal to close Kilrenny School was not accepted by the Board of Education…*they had difficulty in giving their sanction to the abandonment of the Public School in Kilrenny which is in good condition and capable of accepting 149 children and is also locally convenient for the landward part of the parish.* Eventually the majority of children attended Cellardyke School. By 1937 the instruction of children from 5 to 9 in one schoolroom was regarded as an unacceptable anachronism and the school was closed.

CELLARDYKE SCHOOL

Until 1878 the children of Cellardyke were educated in Female and Infant Schools and in the school at Kilrenny. After a review of the school population the School Board proposed a central school for four hundred local children aged from 5 to 13. Two sites were considered and an inspection conducted by Principal Tulloch of St Andrews University in November 1873 determined that the school should be built at the top of Windmill Road, but reasons were found for preferring the site at the corner of Toll Road and West Forth Street. The decision to close Kilrenny School at this time was also rescinded. The new school was opened in 1878. An iron cannonball found during the building of the foundations was exhibited in a glass case in the school for many years.

Cellardyke School

The high reputation that the school has enjoyed for many years was soon established. In May 1888 Her Majesty's Inspector reported that *the tidiness, cheerfulness and faultless behaviour of the children attest to the excellent training they receive. The results were excellent, and in arithmetic could hardly be surpassed. The penmanship was also superior... however the singing was not very tuneful.* 246 pupils were present of whom 182 were presented for examination. On leaving the school each child was presented with a bun.

Absenteeism was a continual problem, particularly in the autumn when children went with their parents to the fishing off Yarmouth or worked on the potato harvest. Lack of boots also prevented attendance during winter months so arrangements were made to provide children with boots and clothes. Comments concerning changeable weather affecting attendance appear in the school records into the '20s.

Cellardyke School has had a successful record over nearly 130 years of preparing pupils for secondary education, principally at the Waid.

THE WAID ACADEMY

Anstruther's Waid Academy was formally opened in September 1886 before a packed school hall by Sir Ralph Anstruther of Balcaskie, The Rev. Thomas Murray, Chairman of the Board of Governors, and Principal Donaldson of St Andrews University, who in his address dwelt at some length on the priceless advantages of Classical Studies. The first Headmaster, R. Bruce Lockhart, was a distinguished Classical scholar, graduate of Edinburgh and Cambridge and senior Classics Master at Merchiston Castle School (founded by Charles, brother of Dr Thomas Chalmers).

This seems a far cry from the will of Lt Waid, RN, of 1800 which envisaged the accommodation, clothing and education of orphan boys and sons of indigent seamen to qualify them as useful sailors for the British Navy.

Andrew Waid died in 1804 leaving his close relatives amply provided for but *the annuitants proved to be extremely long-lived* and it was not until 1860 that sufficient money was available to set up Waid's Orphan Naval Academy. His house in East Green which he had intended for the Academy had already been sold; a new site had to be found and the Navy had by then its own training scheme.

The 1872 Education (Scotland) Act made education compulsory for all children from 5 to 13 years of age and free for needy children. The School Boards set up for the purpose were financed by the rates, fees of up to 9d per pupil and most pertinent for the future of the Waid, from endowments, with strict adherence to the purpose laid down by the donor.

Anstruther Easter's School Board interpreted Waid's bequest as a Donation to promote Higher Education, thus freeing money for their provision of Elementary Education. But had not Waid's aim been to benefit the British Navy? The School Board argued that it had been primarily to benefit his native town.

After, one suspects much wrangling, the Admiralty agreed in 1877 to go along with the Easter School Board by passing the *Waid's Orphan Academy Act* and later the *Endowment Institutions (Scotland) Act* which made changes to the original Trust Deed possible.

In 1882 the Burleigh Committee was set up to enable the Waid Academy (*Orphans* no longer) to be established as a fee-paying secondary school for boys and girls, with fees and books available free to those poor children who had achieved a satisfactory standard of elementary education. Moreover the school was to serve not only the combined burghs but also pupils from Crail to the East and Largo to the West (thanks to the presence of the Leven-Dundee railway)

An acre of ground between Adelaide Lodge and the railway was chosen as the site for the new school. The architect was David Henry of St Andrews, later to design Chalmers' Memorial Church.

There were 4 classrooms and a hall. Above the main entrance is a carving of a sailing ship between two towers and the school motto beneath *Multi per transibunt et augebitur Scientia* (many will pass through and knowledge will increase). From the tower, the gift of Stephen Williamson, the school flag is flown on special occasions including Waid's birthday, 18th June.

The Waid Academy

The aim of the new school was to provide a liberal education for boys and girls above the age of 10 who passed the entrance exam. The school hours were to be from 9.15 am to 4.00 pm with an interval. *These hours have been fixed to suit both east and west trains.* The fees per quarter were *£1 for the first and second classes, and £1 10s for senior classes. Pianoforte £1 1s extra.*

From the first year Waid was a success. The Rev. Thomas Murray put it down to the inspirational headmaster, Bruce Lockhart.

It is interesting to note that evening classes in arithmetic, French, and German for the general public were initiated in the first year and proved a success. On a greatly increased scale and with a great variety of vocational subjects Waid still provides this resource for the community.

Up to 1986 navigation was still in the curriculum but when Mr Bill Muir retired he proved to be irreplaceable. Classics, on the other hand, is still on offer, together with new subjects required by the age such as computer studies. So *The Waid*, as it is generally and affectionately known continues to adapt to the needs of the community which it serves.

The rector's house was designed by the same architect and at the same time as the school – in fact from outside it is an integral part of the school though it has its own front door. It consisted of 3 public rooms and 5 bedrooms (perhaps to allow for boarders). The last rector to live there with his family was Ian Fraser (1966 – 71). Since then it has provided much needed additional accommodation for the school, for remedial teaching and a room for counselling.

VOCATIONAL TRAINING

Training for work was in the school syllabus even in the early parish schools. As many local boys went to sea navigation, as well as reading writing and Latin, was taught at Anstruther Wester as recorded in the 1845 New Statistical Account. *As the schoolmaster is esteemed the best teacher of navigation on the coast his chief attention is directed to that branch.*

Mr George Dalrymple was appointed to Kilrenny School in 1862 to teach navigation in addition to the usual subjects. Cellardyke

School had Alexander Moncrieff. He was born in 1790 and as a young man had befriended an old sea captain, Robert Lothian, who passed on to him all his knowledge of the sea and navigation. Unable to go to sea because of ill health Alexander became a schoolmaster and is said to have coached more master mariners than any other teacher on the Fife coast.

On going to sea a boy started as ship's cook. The Cellardyke School Inspector in his report of May 1908 hoped that some practical instruction would be provided for older pupils and suggested that in a community like Cellardyke *cookery would be an appropriate subject for both sexes.* By September we read *Cookery has made a good start being taught in 3 divisions of 18 pupils each, both boys and girls taking the work.*

Alongside academic and arts subjects Waid Academy taught navigation, mechanics, needlework, cookery, laundry and woodwork. In the annual report of 1936 we read *A course in navigation suitable for boys proceeding to sea has been developed on good lines... boys often worked well in cookery but too much time was given to baking and using the oven, other methods should be chosen.*

The Anstruther Easter School Board in January 1911 considered possible sites for a separate technical school: at a cost of £1,052 1s 10d with a government grant of £200 the School Boards finally erected the technical school in Ladywalk. Mr George Walker from Edinburgh was appointed to teach woodwork and Miss Stewart from Pittenweem to teach cookery and laundry. The school building is now the Ladywalk Health Centre.

For many years in the local schools girls have been taught sewing and knitting. *Domestic industry is well taught* the Cellardyke School Inspector reported in 1879. Until the early 20th century domestic service was one of the largest areas of female employment. It had the advantage of providing bed and board and an element of career structure: promotion to lady's maid, cook or housekeeper. The local fishing industry also provided employment for girls, but often domestic service, despite the long hours, was considered more congenial than fish gutting or factory work.

CULTURAL AND SOCIAL ACTIVITIES

Gentlemen's clubs flourished in the 18th century and Anstruther eventually had two which became well known beyond the borders of Fife. The first was founded in 1732 by John McNaughton, last hereditary chief of Clan McNaughton and Collector of His Majesties Customs at Anstruther.

The 33 Knights of the Most Ancient Order of the Beggars' Benison under their Sovereign met at Candlemass and on St Andrews Day in a room named the Temple in the old castle of Dreel at the foot of Wightman's Wynd. The founder members were all from the East Neuk: merchants, a shipmaster and shipbuilder, magistrates and local lairds, to be joined later by Scottish peers. The honour of knighthood was bestowed on Vincente Lunardi, the balloonist who landed near Cupar in 1785 and on the Grand Duke Nicholas of Russia in 1819—a chapter of the Order had been founded in St Petersburg in 1773.

The Club was originally of a bawdy nature in the fashion of the time, but it seems to have soon become *a convivial club of distinguished and clever men addicted to literature.* It outlived all the Rakes' Clubs of the 18th century and met for the last time on 30th November 1836.

In about 1812, when his *Anster Fair* was published, William Tennant, West Anstruther's poet, with Capt. Charles Grey RM, John Dow the schoolmaster, William Cockburn the Shore Street bookseller and other local *poetical wits* founded the Musomanik Society. The members met to *ryme and scribble* and to make merry with words. It had a high reputation, including among its members Walter Scott and James Hogg. The *joyous celebrations* of the worthy Society which produced some amusing verse and clever *bouts-rimes*, (end-rhymes) were suspended in 1817 as its principal founders and members separated and dispersed into life's *tumults and unpoetical business.*

David Lumsden in his *Reminiscences of Kilrenny* recalls the more informal intellectual gatherings in his native village at the time of the 1832 Reform Bill. First his father and a neighbour *gloating* over the *Scotsman* in those momentous days, then the local worthies gathering in the shoemaker's shop or the smithy for their nightly discussion, and an important link in the social life of the village, the *evening gathering of cronies in the weaver's shop* met *to lay aside all private cares and mind the Kirk and State affairs.*

Kilrenny also boasted a thriving Debating Society and a Newspaper Club, at the quarterly meetings of which the village laureate, James M'Gill, generally had a song of his own composition prepared for the occasion.

There was a Musical Association in Anstruther run by Dr MacArthur of *Elm Lodge*. It used to practise in the Free Church School in the Back Dykes. When this became the East School the School Board agreed unanimously in December 1873 to allow the arrangement to continue providing the Association paid for the gas used *at the rate of 7/6 for the session..* That year in the newly erected Town Hall in School Green the Association gave its fourth concert, Handel's *Samson* with a choir of 100 voices. In 1892 the choir became the Anstruther Philharmonic Society, which continues to perform its annual concert in the Town Hall.

The Anstruther and District Amateur Operatic Society was founded in 1938 and continues to give annual performances in the Waid school hall and there is a local theatrical association, *The Guizards*. For many years the Women's Burgh Guild flourished, in late years organising a small bus to collect members form one end of the United Burgh to the other for its meetings in the Wester Town Hall. The Kilrenny W.R.I. Continues to flourish in all its many and varied interests and the R.N.L.I. Ladies never cease in their vigorous support for the lifeboat crew. In 1950 the Anstruther Improvements Association, founded to promote general improvements within the United Burghs. Along with fund-raising events it provides a stimulating series of *Anster Nichts*.

Popular readings, meetings of societies and even dancing classes were held in the Wester Town Hall in the 19th century. In Anster's manufacturing days works outings were popular occasions as were the summer Sunday School picnics in places like Craw Hill woods. From the time of William Cockburn until the building of the Murray Library in 1908 there had been a circulating library and reading room in the town and there is still no lack of cultural and social activity, including a new East Neuk Art Club which meets weekly in the Erskine Hall.

SOURCES AND REFERENCES

Anson, Peter: *Underground Catholicism in Scotland* Montrose 1970

Beale, James: *A History of the Burgh and Parochial Schools of Fife*, Nelson 1958

East Neuk Church Group: *A Pictish Trail through Fife*, 1998

Eggeling, W.J.: *The Isle of May*, Oliver and Boyd 1960

Fife Council Library, Cardendon: Headteachers' *Logbooks for Cellardyke School and The Waid Academy*

Fife Council Library, Markinch: *School Board Minute Books*

Gourlay, George: *Anstruther or Illustrations of Scottish Burgh Life* 1888

Grant, James: *History of the Burgh and Parish Schools of Scotland* Collins 1876

Johnson, Christine: *Developments in the Roman Catholic Church in Scotland 1789-1829* John Donald 1983

Knox M.M.: *250 years of Scottish Education* Oliver & Boyd 1953

Mc Roberts, David, ed: *Essays on the Scottish Reformation 1513– 1625* Burns 1962

Smout, T.C.: *History of the Scottish People 1560-1830* Collins 1969

Statistical Account of Scotland 1791-98 Vol III Anstruther

Stevenson, Stephanie: *A History of Anstruther* John Donald 1989

Burgh & Kirk Session Records, University of St Andrews Library

Waid *Magpie*, Waid Academy: *1872 and a ' that* 1972

Watson, Harry: *Kilrenny and Cellardyke* John Donald 1986

Wood, Walter: *The East Neuk of Fife* Oliver & Boyd 1862

We should also like to thank Mr Corstorphine, Dr John Frew, Mr Alec Parker, Rev. Hamish MacNab and Rev. Wm D. McNaughton